CALVINISM

IN THE LIGHT OF SCRIPTURE

A Study by Jeff Archer

ONESTONE
BIBLICAL RESOURCES

Published by:
One Stone Press
979 Lovers Lane
Bowling Green, KY 42103

Printed in the United States of America

ISBN 10: 978-1941422-05-2
ISBN 13: 1-941422-05-5

Supplemental Materials Available:
➢ Answer Key
➢ Downloadable PDF

ONE STONE
BIBLICAL RESOURCES

www.onestone.com
1(800)428-0121

CONTENTS

INTRODUCTION AND OVERVIEW

Historical Background

In the 5th century two men, Pelagius and Augustine, and their teachings were at odds. Pelagius believed that man had the freedom to choose good and evil. His favorite maxim was "If I ought, I can." Augustine believed every part of man—body, soul, and will—was totally depraved, inclined toward evil. Man was incapable of choosing good or even wanting to serve God. As the Catholic Church emerged, it followed the teaching of Augustine. Believing man was born with original sin and incapable of doing anything good, the Catholic Church claimed to be the infuser of grace. Christening an infant took away the stain of sin and then the Church, through its sacraments, infused grace which enabled the person to keep God's law. The more sacraments (good works) one did, the more grace he received to have more power to do even more good.

As the years passed, the traditions of the Catholic Church accumulated and slowly buried the teaching of Augustine. The Catholic Church became increasingly powerful and corrupt in whom it deemed worthy to receive the infusion of the grace of God. Theologians see this period, from the seventh to the sixteenth centuries, as the dark ages. It was "dark" because "there are but few of the many who toiled in this field who added a single essential principle, or furnished a single original contribution to the explanation of the Word of God" (Farrar 245).

John Calvin (1509-1564), a Catholic monk, wrote his *Institutes of the Christian Religion* in 1536 in which he sought to reestablish the teachings of Augustine in the Catholic Church. Calvin further developed and systematized the teachings of Augustine. The Catholic Church would not be reformed. John Calvin fled to Geneva, Switzerland and began his Reformed Church (The Presbyterian Church in the US). Calvin wrote of the reformers of his day, "We may most truly declare that we have brought more light to bear on the understanding of Scripture than all the authors who have sprung up amongst Christians since the rise of the Papacy; nor do they themselves venture to rob us of this praise" (Green 6-7).

Martin Luther, a contemporary of John Calvin, sought to reform the Catholic Church in Germany. Luther also saw the abuses of Catholic teaching and went to the opposite extreme coming to many of the same conclusions as Calvin. The Catholic Church would not be reformed, so Luther and his followers fought for and established a national religion in Germany which became known as the Lutheran Church.

"Of the two theologies which composed the Reformation, Calvinism far surpassed Lutheranism in its ability to inspire the writing of national creeds and confessions. It took root in such diverse countries as Scotland, England, Switzerland, France, Poland, Hungary, the Palatinate, and even in Italy, the home of the Papacy...This influence of Calvinism was not confined to those churches which consciously adopted the Reformed theology in all its parts. It was also the inspiration of the Puritan movement within the Church of England during the seventeenth century, and it lay at the very heart of the English Baptist theology. It also found a home among the English Congregationalists in the Savoy Confession of 1658" (Singer 20-22). There were those who opposed Calvin's teachings such as the Frenchman, Amyraut, who taught "hypothetical universalism" and Arminianism which arose in the Netherlands. The lasting impact, however, on the denominational world is decidedly Calvinistic.

In fact, Calvinism is having a modern day resurgence among a variety of denominations. For example, "about 10 percent of Southern Baptist leaders identify themselves as five-point Calvinists, while about 30 percent of recent seminary graduates identify themselves as such" (Revell 3).

1. Why is it important for us to understand the teaching of Calvinism? _____
_____
_____
_____

Calvinism as Defined by Calvinists

The Sovereignty of God

"The basic principle of Calvinism is the sovereignty of God. This represents the purpose of the Triune of God as absolute and unconditional, independent of the whole finite creation, and originating solely in the eternal counsel of His will. He appoints the course of nature and directs the course of history down to the minutest details. His decrees therefore are eternal, unchangeable, holy wise, and sovereign. They are represented as being the basis of the divine foreknowledge of all future events, and not conditioned by that foreknowledge or by anything originating in the events themselves" (Boettner. "The Sovereignty of God" 6).

TULIP

T – Total Depravity

"Original sin, then, may be defined as a hereditary corruption and depravity of our nature, extending to all parts of the soul, which first makes us obnoxious to the wrath of God, and then produces in us works which in Scripture are termed works of the flesh. This corruption is repeatedly designated by Paul by the term sin (Gal. v.19)..." (Calvin's Institutes, Book 2, Chap. 1, No. 8, page 157).

"Our first parents, being seduced by the subtlety and temptation of Satan, sinned in eating the forbidden fruit. This their sin, God was pleased, according to his wise and holy counsel, to permit, having purposed to order it to his own glory. By this sin they fell from their original righteousness and communion with God, and so became dead in sin, and wholly defiled in all the faculties and parts of the soul and body. They being the root of all mankind, the guilt of this sin was imputed and the same death in sin and corrupted nature conveyed to all their posterity descending from them by ordinary generation. From this original corruption, whereby we are utterly indisposed, disabled, and made opposite to all good, and wholly inclined to all evil, do proceed all actual transgressions" (The Constitution of the Presbyterian Church 195).

U - Unconditional Election
(or Calvinistic Predestination)

"God from all eternity did by the most wise and holy counsel of his own will freely and unchangeably ordained whatsoever comes to pass...By the decree of God, for the manifestation of his glory, some men and angels are predestinated unto life, and others foreordained to everlasting death. These angels and men, thus predestinated and foreordained, are particularly and unchangeably designed; and their number is so certain and definite that it cannot be either increased or diminished" (The Constitution of the Presbyterian Church 192-193).

L – Limited Atonement

"Christ's redeeming work was intended to save the elect only and actually secured salvation for them...In addition to putting away the sins of His people, Christ's redemption secured everything necessary for their salvation, including faith, which united them to Him. The gift of faith is infallibly applied by the Spirit to all for whom Christ died, thereby guaranteeing their salvation" (Steele 17).

I – Irresistible Grace

"Although the general outward call of the gospel can be, and often is, rejected, the special inward call of the Spirit never fails to result in the conversion of those to whom it is made. This special call is not made to all sinners but is issued to the elect only. The Spirit is in no way dependent upon their help or cooperation for success in His work of bringing them to Christ. It is for this reason that Calvinists speak of the Spirit's call and of God's grace in saving sinners as being 'efficacious,' 'invincible,' or 'irresistible.' For the grace which the Holy Spirit extends to the elect cannot be thwarted or refused, it never fails to bring them to true faith in Christ" (Steele 49).

P - Perseverance of the Saints

"Not only does God choose certain ones to be delivered from their total depravity, provide for their salvation and purity, and effectually call them, but He also ordains the means for their preservation in their new life of holiness, righteousness and true knowledge. The indwelling Holy Spirit so preserves and enables that each of the elect most certainly endures to the end" (Green 4).

Questions

2. Beginning with the errors about the sovereignty of God and the depravity of man, does Calvinism follow a logical progression? _____

_____

3. Very few denominations today preach a pure form of Calvinism. Many accept a few points of the teaching. Some are watered down with a lack of conviction. Others are so distracted by their social programs that "Church doctrine" is rarely visible. In the next few weeks we need some volunteers from this class to contact different denominational churches or friends to ask in which points of Calvinism they are in agreement. What church or friend will you contact? _____

_____

4. List examples of the influence of Calvinism you have seen. _____

_____

_____

_____

THE SOVEREIGNTY OF GOD
As Defined By Calvinists

The Sovereignty of God

"If one falls among robbers, or ravenous beasts; if a sudden gust of wind at sea causes shipwreck; if one is struck down by the fall of a house or a tree; if another, when wandering through desert paths, meets with deliverance; or, after being tossed by the waves, arrives in port, and makes some wondrous hair-breadth escape from death—all these occurrences, prosperous as well as adverse, carnal sense will attribute to fortune. But whose has learned from the mouth of Christ that all the hairs of his head are numbered (Matt. 10:30), will look farther for the cause, and hold that all events whatsoever are governed by the secret counsel of God" (Calvin's Institutes, Book 1, Chapter 16, No. 2, p. 127).

Benjamin Warfield, a Calvinist, said, "In the infinite wisdom of the Lord of all the earth, each event falls with exact precision into its proper place in the unfolding of His divine plan. Nothing, however small, however strange, occurs without His ordering, or without its particular fitness for its place in the working out of His purpose; and the end of all shall be the manifestation of His glory, and the accumulation of His praise...Therefore, as we shall see, whatever comes to pass in the history of mankind does so by virtue of the fact that it suited the eternal plan or Purpose of God. Should anything take place contrary to the will of God...Then Satan and man (on occasion at least) must be equal or superior to the Creator whose Word claims that He is omnipotent and wholly irresistible! Therefore, whatever comes to pass in any part of creation, at any time in history, does so because the omniscient God knew it as a possibility, willed it as a reality by His omnipotence, and established it in His divine plan or Purpose" (Spencer 21).

The Sovereignty of God and Man's Salvation

"But when once the light of Divine Providence has illumined the believer's soul, he is relieved and set free, not only from the extreme fear and anxiety which formerly oppressed him, but from all care. For as he justly shudders at the idea of chance, so he can confidently commit himself to God. This, I say, is his comfort, that his heavenly Father so embraces all things under his power—so governs them at will by his nod—so regulates them by his wisdom, that nothing takes place save according to his appointment; that received into his favour, and entrusted to the care of his angels neither fire, nor water, nor sword, can do him harm, except in so far as God their master is pleased to permit" (Calvin's Institutes, Book 1, Chapter 17, No. 11, p. 142).

"The basic principle of Calvinism is the sovereignty of God. This represents the purpose of the Triune of God as absolute and unconditional, independent of the whole finite creation, and originating solely in the eternal counsel of His will. He appoints the course of nature and directs the course of history down to the minutest details. His decrees, therefore, are eternal, unchangeable, holy wise, and sovereign. They are represented as being the basis of the divine foreknowledge of all future events, and not conditioned by that foreknowledge or by anything originating in the events themselves" (Boettner, Reformed Doctrine of Predestination 6).

"Salvation is accomplished by the almighty power of the triune God. The Father chose a people, the Son died for them, the Holy Spirit makes Christ's death effective by bringing the elect to faith and repentance, thereby causing them to willingly obey the Gospel. The entire process (election, redemption, regeneration) is the work of God and is by grace alone. Thus God, not man, determines who will be the recipients of the gift of salvation" (Boettner, Reformed Faith 14).

The Sovereignty of God and Man's Will

"To say that God the Father has purposed the salvation of all mankind, that God the Son died with the express intention of saving the whole human race, and that God the Holy Spirit is now seeking to win the world to Christ; when, as a matter of common observation, it is apparent that the great majority of our fellowmen are dying in sin, and passing into a hopeless eternity; is to say that God the Father is disappointed, that God the Son is dissatisfied, and that God the Holy Spirit is defeated. We have stated the issue badly, but there is no escaping the conclusion. To argue that God is 'trying His best' to save all mankind, but that the majority of men will not let Him save them, is to insist that the will of the Creator is impotent, and that the will of the creature is omnipotent" (Pink chapter 1).

"To declare that the Creator's original plan has been frustrated by sin, is to dethrone God. To suggest that God was taken by surprise in Eden and that He is now attempting to remedy an unforeseen calamity, is to degrade the Most High to the level of a finite, erring mortal. To argue that man is a free moral agent and the determiner of his own destiny, and that therefore he has the power to checkmate his Maker, is to strip God of the attribute of Omnipotence...In a word, to deny the Sovereignty of God is to enter upon a path which, if followed to its logical terminus, is to arrive at blank atheism" (Pink chapter 1).

"Men may connive and scheme, following the counter plan of their god, Satan, but they cannot bring to pass so much as one act contrary to the will and plan of God who foreordained all of history from the largest event to the most insignificant" (Spencer 26).

1. According to the Calvinist, how much of what happens on the earth is predetermined by God? _____
_____

2. According to the Calvinist, does man have any role in the salvation of his soul? ___
_____

   a. According to the Calvinist, who does everything to save man's soul? _____
   _____

3. According to the Calvinist, does man have the ability to choose something contrary to the will of God? _____

4. According to the Calvinist, what does "the sovereignty of God" mean? _____
_____

Let's Look At The Scriptures

5. Has God foreknown some events before they happened? _____

   a. What did God know Pharaoh would do (Exod. 7:4-5)? _____
   _____

   b. What did God know Judas would do (John 6:64; 13:1, 2, 11, 18-27)? _____
   _____

   c. Did God force these events to happen? _____

6. Has God predetermined some events (in the sense that He caused/forced them to happen according to His will)? _____
_____

   a. What did God cause to happen with Abraham and Sarah (Gen. 18:9-14)? _____
   _____

   b. What was going to happen to the temple? Did God cause the destruction (Matt. 24:2)? _____
   _____

   c. What part did God play in the death of Jesus (Acts 2:22-23)? _____
   _____

   d. When did the plan for Jesus to die originate (1 Pet. 1:20)? _____
   _____

     * Did Jesus have a choice (John 10:17-18)? _____

7. Has God predetermined everything that happens? _____

   a. Do all men repent (2 Pet. 3:9)? _____

   b. Are all men saved (1 Tim. 2:4)? _____

   c. Is everything that happens according to the will of God? _____
   _____

THE SOVEREIGNTY OF GOD (2)

Lets Look at the Scriptures (continued)

1. Has God ever changed His will in response to something man has done? _____
_____

   a. What did God say He was going to do to the children of Israel? What changed
     His will (Exod. 32:10-14)? _____
     _____

   b. What did God say would happen to Nineveh? What changed His mind (Jonah
     3:4-10)? _____
     _____

Regarding Jonah 4:10, Calvin said in his commentary,

> "We hence see that there is a twofold view of God,—as he sets himself
> forth in his word,—and as he is as to his hidden counsel. With regard
> to his secret counsel, I have already said that God is always like himself,
> and is subject to none of our feelings: but with regard to the teaching
> of his word, it is accommodated to our capacities. God is now angry
> with us, and then, as though he were pacified, he offers pardon, and
> is propitious to us. Such is the repentance of God.
>
> Let us then remember that it proceeds from his word, that God is
> said to repent; for the Ninevites could form no other opinion but
> that it was God's decree that they were to be destroyed,—how so?
> because he had so testified by his word. But when they rose up to an
> assurance of deliverance, they then found that a change had taken
> place, that is, according to the knowledge of their own faith: and the
> feelings both of fear and of joy proceeded from the word: for when
> God denounced his wrath, it was necessary for the wretched men to
> be terrified; but when he invited them to a state of safety by propos-
> ing reconciliation to them, he then put on a new character; and thus
> they ascribed a new feeling to God. This is the meaning."

   c. In what way are our prayers effective (James 5:16)? _____
     _____

2. Does man have any role in salvation? _____

   a. Besides grace, what is necessary for salvation (Eph. 2:8-9)? _____
   _____

   b. Who does this, God or man? _____

   c. Will man be saved if he will not do what Jesus says in Mark 16:15-16? _____

   d. What does "if" mean (Col.1:22-23)? _____
   _____

3. Does man have the ability to choose whether he will obey God or rebel against His
   will? _____

   a. What did man do against God's will (Rom. 1:20-23)? _____
   _____

   b. What did some choose to do in response to the gospel (Acts 2:37-41)? _____
   _____

   c. What is free will? _____
   _____

4. How can God be sovereign and man have the ability to reject Him? _____

   a. Can a man sin against God and "get away with it" (Gal. 6:7-8)? _____
   _____

   b. To whom will we answer for our actions (2 Cor. 5:10)? _____
   _____

   c. What will happen if we reject Jesus (John 12:48)? _____
   _____

TOTAL DEPRAVITY
As Defined By Calvinists

"Original sin, then, may be defined as hereditary corruption and depravity of our nature, extending to all parts of the soul, which first makes us obnoxious to the wrath of God, and then produces in us works which in Scripture are termed works of the flesh. This corruption is repeatedly designated by Paul by the term sin (Gal. v.19)" (Calvin's Institutes, Book 2, Chapter 1, No. 8, p. 157).

"Our first parents, being seduced by the subtlety and temptation of Satan, sinned in eating the forbidden fruit. This their sin, God was pleased, according to his wise and holy counsel, to permit, having purposed to order it to his own glory. By this sin they fell from their original righteousness and communion with God, and so became dead in sin, and wholly defiled in all the faculties and parts of the soul and body. They being the root of all mankind, the guilt of this sin was imputed and the same death in sin and corrupted nature conveyed to all their posterity descending from them by ordinary generation. From this original corruption, whereby we are utterly indisposed, disabled, and made opposite to all good, and wholly inclined to all evil, do proceed all actual transgressions" (Presbyterian Confession of Faith).

"You must hold five distinct beliefs in order to affirm Augustinian anthropology. You must believe that everyone behaves in ways that we usually describe as selfish, cruel, arrogant, and so on. You must believe that we are hard-wired to behave in those ways and not do so simply because of the bad examples of others. You must believe that such behavior is properly called wrong or sinful, whether it's evolutionarily adaptive or not. You must believe that it was not originally in our nature to behave in such a way, but that we have fallen from a primal innocence. And you must believe that only supernatural intervention, in the form of what Christians call grace, is sufficient to drag us up out of this pit we've dug for ourselves" (Jacobs 269-270).

Total Depravity As Defined By Related Denominations

Roman Catholic

"Still, the transmission of original sin is a mystery that we cannot fully understand. But we do know by Revelation that Adam had received original holiness and justice not for himself alone, but for all human nature. By yielding to the tempter, Adam and Eve committed a personal sin, but this sin affected the human nature that they would then transmit in a fallen state. It is a sin which will be transmitted by propagation to all mankind, that is, by the transmission of a human nature deprived of original holiness and justice...It is a sin 'contracted' and not 'committed'—a state not an act...It is a deprivation of original holiness and justice, but human nature has not been totally corrupted: it is wounded in the natural powers proper to it; subject to ignorance, suffering, and the domination of death; and inclined to sin—an inclination to evil that is called 'concupiscence'" (Catholic Catechism 102).

Lutheran

"It is also taught among us that since the fall of Adam all men who are born according to the course of nature are conceived and born in sin. That is, all men are full of evil lust and inclination from their mother's womb and are unable by nature to have true fear of God and true faith in God. Moreover, this inborn sickness and hereditary sin is truly sin and condemns to the eternal wrath of God all whose who are not born again through baptism and the Holy Spirit" (Augsburg Confession Article 2).

Methodist (Anglican/Episcopal have the same belief)

"Original sin standeth not in the following of Adam (as the Pelagians do vainly talk), but it is the corruption of the nature of every man, that naturally is engendered of the offspring of Adam, whereby man is very far gone from original righteousness, and of his own nature inclined to evil, and that continually" (The Book of Discipline 67).

"The condition of man after the fall of Adam is such, that he cannot turn and prepare himself, by his own natural strength and works, to faith, and calling upon God; wherefore we have no power to do good work, pleasant and acceptable to God, without the grace of God by Christ preventing us, that we may have a good will, and working with us, when we have that good will" (The Book of Discipline 67).

Church of the Nazarene

"We believe that sin came into the world through the disobedience of our first parents, and death by sin. We believe that sin is of two kinds: original sin or depravity, and actual or personal sin. We believe that original sin, or depravity, is that corruption of the nature of all the offspring of Adam by reason of which everyone is very far gone from the original righteousness or the pure state of our first parents at the time of their creation, is averse to God, is without spiritual life, and inclined to evil, and that continually. We further believe that original sin continues to exist with the new life of the regenerate, until eradicated by the baptism with the Holy Spirit. We believe that original sin differs from actual sin in that it constitutes an inherited propensity to actual sin for which no one is accountable until its divinely provided remedy is neglected or rejected" (Church of the Nazarene Manual 26).

Christian and Missionary Alliance

"Man was Originally created in the image and likeness of God; he fell through disobedience, incurring thereby both physical and spiritual death. All men are born with a sinful nature, are separated from the life of God, and can be saved only through the atoning work of the Lord Jesus Christ" (Manual, Statement of faith Article III # 5).

Pentecostal

"Man was Originally created in the image and likeness of God. He fell through sin, and as a consequence, incurred both spiritual and physical death. Spiritual death and the depravity of human nature have been transmitted to the entire human race with the exception of the Man Jesus. Man can be saved only through the atoning work of the Lord Jesus Christ" (Statement of Fundamental and Essential Truths Pentecostal Assemblies of Canada 3).

Baptist

"We believe the Scriptures teach that a man was created in holiness, under the law of his Maker; but by voluntary transgression fell from that holy and happy state; in consequence of which all mankind are now sinners not by constraint but choice; being by nature utterly void of that holiness required by the law of God, positively inclined to evil; and therefore under just condemnation, without defense or excuse" (Hiscox 60).

Let's Look At The Scriptures

1. Man has two parts to his nature: a spirit made in the image of God and a flesh made of the material world.

   a. Our spirit, since it is in the image of God, can discern between what is morally good and what is evil. In what does the spirit delight (Rom. 7:22)? _____
   _____

   b. What will we find if we choose to walk according to the spirit (Rom. 8:5-6)? _____
   _____
   _____

   c. Can our flesh, which is made up of desires and passions, discern what is good and what is evil (Rom. 8:7-8)? _____
   _____

   d. Because of this duel nature, we struggle within ourselves. Is it possible to choose to follow the spirit rather than the flesh (Rom. 8:9)? _____
   _____

   e. Is there any time when a temptation will be so strong that we cannot resist it (1 Cor. 10:13)? _____
   _____

2. Satan influenced Eve and then Adam to eat of the forbidden fruit. His approach with us today is much the same as his approach was then. The difference is that they lived in an innocent world unstained by sin and we live in a world where we see sin and its affect all around us.

   a. When Satan approached Eve, what did he say to deceive her spirit's sense of right and wrong (Gen. 3:1-5)? _____
   _____
   _____

   b. How did Eve's flesh react to the fruit (Gen. 3:6)? _____
   _____
   _____

3. What does "through one man sin entered the world" mean (Rom. 5:12)? _____
   _____

   a. Upon what condition do we inherit spiritual death (Rom. 5:12)? _____
   _____

   b. When God listed the consequences for the sin of Adam and Eve, what were the consequences for women (Gen. 3:16)? _____
   _____
   _____

   c. What were the consequences for men (Gen. 3:17-19)? _____
   _____

   d. What were the consequences for mankind (Gen. 3:23-24)? _____
   _____

   e. Is there any mention of an "hereditary corruption" or "depravity of our nature?" __
   _____

In his commentary on Romans 5:12, Calvin said, "For as Adam at his creation had received for us as well as for himself the gifts of God's favor, so by falling away from the Lord, he in himself corrupted, vitiated, depraved, and ruined our nature; for having been divested of God's likeness, he could not have generated seed but what was like himself. Hence we have all sinned; for we are all imbued with natural corruption, and so are become sinful and wicked. Frivolous then was the gloss, by which formerly the Pelagians endeavored to elude the words of Paul, and held, that sin descended by imitation from Adam to the whole human race;...It then follows that our innate and hereditary depravity is what is here referred to."

4. The first 3 chapters of Romans prove that all men are sinners. Paul sums up his argument in 3:23, "for all have sinned and fall short of the glory of God." How did he prove that all men are sinners? Did Paul say that man inherited sin or did he talk about the actual personal choices to sin? _____
   _____
   _____

a. Were these men sinners because they inherited Adam's sin or because they personally chose to do wrong (Rom. 1:20-23)? _____

_____

b. Why were the Jews sinners (Rom. 2:21-23)? _____

_____

c. Did man go out of "the way" because Adam did or because each man made his own choice (Rom. 3:10-12)? _____

_____

TOTAL DEPRAVITY (2)

As Defined By Calvinists

Let's Look at the Scriptures

1. In the midst of a sinful environment, how did Noah find favor in the eyes of God (Gen. 6:5,8; Heb. 11:7)? _____
_____

2. In what sense was David "brought forth in iniquity and in sin my mother conceived me" (Psa. 51:5)? _____
_____

Calvin said in his commentary on Ezekiel 18:20, "If then we are children of wrath, it follows that we are polluted from our birth; this provokes God's anger and renders him hostile to us: in this sense David confesses himself conceived in sin (Psalms 51:5). He does not here accuse either his father or his mother so as to extenuate his own wickedness; but, when he abhors the greatness of his sin in provoking the wrath of God, he is brought back to his infancy, and acknowledges that he was even then guilty before God. We see then that David, being reminded of a single sin, acknowledges himself a sinner before he was born; and since we are all under the curse, it follows that we are all worthy of death."

3. What was the complaint of the Israelites (Ezek. 18:2)? _____
_____

4. Is God sovereign (Ezek. 18:4)? _____
_____

5. Who will live (Ezek. 18:5-9)? _____
_____

6. Who will die (Ezek. 18:10-13)? _____
_____

7. Who will live (Ezek. 18:14-17)? _____
_____

8. Put Ezek. 18:20 in your own words. _____
_____

Calvin also said in his commentary on Ezekiel 18:20, "Now therefore it is evident how God throws the iniquity of the fathers upon the children, since when he devoted both father and son to eternal destruction, he deprives them of all his gifts, blinds their minds, and enslaves all their appetites to the devil...But how will this now be suitable, 'shall not the son bear the iniquity of the father?' for Ezekiel here speaks of adults, for he means that the son shall not bear his father's iniquity, since he shall receive his reward due to himself and sustain his own burden. Should any one wish to strive with God, he can be refuted in a single word: for who can boast himself innocent? Since therefore all are guilty through their own fault, it follows that the son does not bear his father's iniquity, since he has to bear his own at the same time. Now that question is solved."

9. Can a man change? Can a sinner choose to do right? Can a righteous man choose to do evil (Ezek. 18:21-24)? _____
   _____

10. David's son, who was born as a result of his adultery with Bathsheba, died. Did David believe his son inherited the original sin or his sin of adultery (2 Sam. 12:23)?
    _____
    _____

11. Did Jesus see children as sinners (Matt. 18:2-5; 19:14)? _____
    _____

In his commentary on Matthew 19:14 Calvin said, "He declares that he wishes to receive children; and at length, taking them in his arms, he not only embraces, but blesses them by the laying on of hand; from which we infer that his grace is extended even to those who are of that age. And no wonder; for since the whole race of Adam is shut up under the sentence of death, all from the least even to the greatest must perish, except those who are rescued by the only Redeemer. To exclude from the grace of redemption those who are of that age would be too cruel; and therefore it is not without reason that we employ this passage as a shield against the Anabaptists. They refuse baptism to infants, because infants are incapable of understanding that mystery which is denoted by it. We, on the other hand, maintain that, since baptism is the pledge and figure of the forgiveness of sins, and likewise of adoption by God, it ought not to be denied to infants, whom God adopts and washes with the blood of his Son. Their objection, that repentance and newness of life are also denoted by it, is easily answered. Infants are renewed by the Spirit of God, according to the capacity of their age, till that power which was concealed within them grows by degrees, and becomes fully manifest at the proper time."

12. Whom did Jesus want to be baptized (Mark 16:15-16)? _____
    _____

13. If all men inherit the sin of Adam, was Jesus a sinner (Heb. 2:17; 4:15)? _____
    _____

<u>U</u>NCONDITIONAL ELECTION

As Defined By Calvinists

Unconditional Election or Predestination

"God from all eternity did by the most wise and holy counsel of his own will freely and unchangeably ordain whatsoever comes to pass...By the decree of God, for the manifestation of his glory, some men and angels are predestinated unto life, and others foreordained to everlasting death. These angels and men, thus predestinated and foreordained, are particularly and unchangeably designed; and their number is so certain and definite that it cannot be either increased or diminished" (The Constitution of the Presbyterian Church 192).

"The doctrine of election declares that God, before the foundation of the world, chose certain individuals from among the fallen members of Adam's race to be the objects of His undeserved favor. These, and these only, He purposed to save. God could have chosen to save all men (for He had the power and authority to do so) or He could have chosen to save none (for He was under no obligation to show mercy to any)—but He did neither. Instead He chose to save some and to exclude others. His eternal choice of particular sinners unto salvation was not based upon any foreseen act or response on the part of those selected, but was based solely on His own good pleasure and sovereign will. Thus election was not determined by, or conditioned upon, anything that men would do, but resulted entirely from God's self-determined purpose" (Steele 30).

"Those who were not chosen to salvation were passed by and left to their own evil devices and choices. It is not within the creature's jurisdiction to call into question the justice of the Creator for not choosing every one to salvation. It is enough to know that the Judge of the earth has done right. It should, however, be kept in mind that if God had not graciously CHOSEN A PEOPLE FOR Himself and sovereignly determined to PROVIDE salvation for them and APPLY it to them, none would be saved. The fact that He did this for some, to the exclusion of others, is in no way unfair to the latter group, unless of course one maintains that God was under obligation to provide salvation for sinners—a position which the Bible utterly rejects." (Steele 31)

Calvin believed in "double predestination" that is, he believed that God predestined some specific individuals for salvation and other specific individuals for condemnation. Martin Luther struggled with this idea. He believed in "single predestination" that is, God unconditionally chose some specific individuals for salvation but did not pre-destine specific individuals to be condemned. Luther said, "Is it not against all natural reason that God out of his mere whim deserts men, hardens them, damns them, as if he delighted in sins and in such torments of the wretched for eternity, he who is said to be of such mercy and goodness? This appears iniquitous, cruel, and intolerable in God, by which very many have been offended in all ages. And who would not be? I was myself more than once driven to the very abyss of despair so that I wished I had never been created. Love God? I hated him!" (Bainton 59).

Unconditional Election As Defined By Universalists
(This would be the opposite extreme of the Calvinists in application.)

"In the seventeenth and eighteenth centuries, radical reformers in Europe and America also studied the Bible closely. They found only a few references to hell, which they believed orthodox Christians had grossly misinterpreted. They found, both in the Bible and in their own hearts, an unconditionally loving God. They believed that God would not deem any human being unworthy of divine love, and that salvation was for all. Because of this emphasis on universal salvation, they called themselves Universalists.

"In the eighteenth century, a dogmatic Calvinist insistence on predestination and human depravity seemed to liberal Christians irrational, perverse, and contrary to both biblical tradition and immediate experience. Liberal Christians believe that human beings are free to heed an inner summons of conscience and character. To deny human freedom is to make God a tyrant and to undermine God-given human dignity" (Wesley 2).

Let's Look At The Scriptures

1. Does God want some men or all men to be saved (1 Tim. 2:3-4)? _____
_____

2. Is God a "respecter of persons" (Rom. 2:11; Acts 10:34)? _____
_____

3. Paul said that the Thessalonians were "chosen" by God and "called" by Him in 2 Thessalonians 2:13-14. How were they called? _____
_____

4. The Calvinists use Ephesians 1:4-5 as a proof text. They point to the word "predes-tined" or "foreordained" and say that the saved were individually elected before the foundation of the world.

   a. What does "predestined" mean? _____
   _____

   b. What did God "predestine"? Individuals or a group? _____
   _____

c. Is being included in this group conditional or unconditional (Eph. 2:4-9)? (Please note: If man must choose to meet any condition for salvation, Calvinism is error.)

_____

_____

5. The Calvinists use Romans 9:10-13 as a proof text. They correctly point out that God chose/elected Jacob over Esau and that this election was not based on the goodness or evil of the boys, but on God's sovereignty. The Calvinists, however, incorrectly apply this to the salvation of the elect.

a. Is this passage dealing with the eternal salvation of Jacob and Esau? _____

_____

b. If not, with what is it dealing? _____

_____

6. The Calvinists use Romans 11:5-6 as a proof text. They say the remnant was un-conditionally elected.

a. Who is this remnant? _____

_____

b. Is their inclusion into the church of Christ conditional or unconditional (Rom. 11:11-12)? _____

_____

c. A specific example of the "remnant" would be the 3,000 Jews on the day of Pentecost in Acts 2. Were they saved conditionally or unconditionally (Acts 2:37-41)? _____

_____

LIMITED ATONEMENT

As Defined By Calvinists

Limited Atonement

"Christ's redeeming work was intended to save the elect only and actually secured salvation for them...In addition to putting away the sins of His people, Christ's redemption secured everything necessary for their salvation, including faith, which united them to Him. The gift of faith is infallibly applied by the Spirit to all for whom Christ died, thereby guaranteeing their salvation" (Steele 17).

"It will be seen at once that this doctrine necessarily follows from the doctrine of election. If from eternity God has planned to save one portion of the human race and not another, it seems to be a contradiction to say that His work has equal reference to both portions, or that He sent His son to die for those whom He had predetermined not to save, as truly as, and in the same sense that He was sent to die for those whom He had chosen for salvation. These two doctrines must stand or fall together. We cannot logically accept one and reject the other. If God has elected some and not others to eternal life, then plainly the primary purpose of Christ's work was to redeem the elect" (Boettner, Reformed Doctrine of Predestination 150).

"All Calvinists agree that Christ's obedience and suffering were of infinite value, and that if God had so willed, the satisfaction rendered by Christ would have saved every member of the human race. It would have required no more obedience, nor any greater suffering for Christ to have secured salvation for every man, woman and child who ever lived than it did for Him to secure salvation for the elect only. But He came into the world to represent and save only those given to Him by the Father. Thus Christ's saving work was limited in that it was designed to save some and not others, but it was not limited in value for it was of infinite worth and would have secured salvation for everyone if this had been God's intent" (Steele 39).

Let's Look At The Scriptures

1. The Calvinists use John 10:15 as a proof text. They say that Jesus died for His sheep and only His sheep. Is this true? _____

_____

2. According to John 17:2, 9, 12, 24, upon whom does Jesus want the blessings and protection of the Father to come? _____

_____

Calvin said in his commentary on John 17:9, "Besides, we learn from these words, that God chooses out of the world those whom he thinks fit to choose to be heirs of life, and that this distinction is not made according to the merit of men, but depends on his mere good-pleasure. For those who think that the cause of election is in men must begin with faith. Now, Christ expressly declares that they who are given to him belong to the Father; and it is certain that they are given so as to believe, and that faith flows from this act of giving. If the origin of faith is this act of giving, and if election comes before it in order and time, what remains but that we acknowledge that those whom God wishes to be saved out of the world are elected by free grace? Now since Christ prays for the elect only, it is necessary for us to believe the doctrine of election, if we wish that he should plead with the Father for our salvation. A grievous injury, therefore, is inflicted on believers by those persons who endeavor to blot out the knowledge of election from the hearts of believers, because they deprive them of the pleading and intercession of the Son of God."

3. According to John 3:16, to whom has God offered salvation? _____

_____

Calvin said in his commentary on John 3:16, "Both points are distinctly stated to us: namely, that faith in Christ brings life to all, and that Christ brought life, because the Heavenly Father loves the human race, and wishes that they should not perish. And this order ought to be carefully observed; for such is the wicked ambition which belongs to our nature, that when the question relates to the origin of our salvation, we quickly form diabolical imaginations about our own merits. Accordingly, we imagine that God is reconciled to us, because he has reckoned us worthy that he should look upon us. But Scripture everywhere extols his pure and unmingled mercy, which sets aside all merits...Let us remember, on the other hand, that while life is promised universally to all who believe in Christ, still faith is not common to all. For Christ is made known and held out to the view of all, but the elect alone are they whose eyes God opens, that they may seek him by faith."

4. For whom did Jesus die (1 John 2:2)? _____

Calvin in his commentary on 1 John 2:2 says, "Here a question may be raised, how have the sins of the whole world been expiated? I pass by the dotages of the fanatics, who under this pretense extend salvation to all the reprobate, and therefore to Satan himself. Such a monstrous thing deserves no refutation. They who seek to avoid this absurdity, have said that Christ suffered sufficiently for the whole world, but efficiently only for the elect. This solution has commonly prevailed in the schools. Though then I allow that what has been said is true, yet I deny that it is suitable to this passage; for the design of John was no other than to make this benefit common to the whole Church. Then under the word all or whole, he does not include the reprobate, but designates those who should believe as well as those who were then scattered through various parts of the world."

5. Whom did the Father send the Son to save (1 John 4:14)? _____
   _____

6. For whom did Jesus die (John 1:29)? _____
   _____

7. For whom did Jesus die (Heb. 2:9-10)? _____
   _____

8. Did Jesus die for only a select few (1 Tim. 2:5-6)? _____
   _____

9. Does God enjoy seeing the wicked remain in their sins (Ezek. 18:23, 32)? _____
   _____

10. Whom did Jesus come to save (Luke 19:10)? _____

11. Whom did Jesus want to hear the gospel (Mark 16:15-16)? _____
    _____

IRRESISTIBLE GRACE

As Defined By Calvinists

Irresistible Grace or Direct Operation of the Holy Spirit

Regarding irresistible grace, consider the following statements from the Westminster Confession of Faith.

> II. This effectual call is of God's free and special grace alone, not from anything at all foreseen in man, who is altogether passive therein, until, being quickened and renewed by the Holy Spirit, he is thereby enabled to answer this call, and to embrace the grace offered and conveyed in it (The Westminster Confession of Faith 47-48).

> III. Elect infants, dying in infancy, are regenerated, and saved by Christ, through the Spirit, who works when, and where, and how He pleases: so also are all other elect persons who are incapable of being outwardly called by the ministry of the Word. (The Westminster Confession of Faith 48-49)

"The HOLY SPIRT, in order to bring God's elect to salvation, extends to them A SPECIAL INWARD CALL in addition to the outward call contained in the gospel message. Through this special call the Holy Spirit performs a work of grace within the sinner which inevitably brings him to faith in Christ. The inward change wrought in the elect sinner enables him to understand and believe spiritual truth; in the spiritual realm he is given the seeing eye and the hearing ear. The Spirit creates within him a new heart or a new nature" (Steele 48).

"Although the general outward call of the gospel can be, and often is, rejected, the special inward call of the Spirit never fails to result in the conversion of those to whom it is made. This special call is not made to all sinners but is issued to the elect only. The Spirit is in no way dependent upon their help or cooperation for success in His work of bringing them to Christ. It is for this reason that Calvinists speak of the Spirit's call and of God's grace in saving sinners as being 'efficacious,' 'invincible,' or 'irresistible.' For the grace which the Holy Spirit extends to the elect cannot be thwarted or refused, it never fails to bring them to true faith in Christ" (Steele 49).

"What is meant when the Calvinist speaks of 'Irresistible Grace'? We answer first in the negative. It does not mean that God does violence to man's spirit by forcing him to do something he does not want to do. (He did not force Judas to do what he did.

Judas acted freely, according to the good pleasure of Satan his master, by doing what his dead human spirit, his sin-corrupted soul, dictated he should do...) Judas, without coercion, fulfilled the will of God.

"'Irresistible', when used of the grace of God toward His elect means that God, of His own free will, gives life to whom He chooses. Since the living human spirit which is 'born of God' finds the Living God wholly irresistible, just as a dead human spirit finds the god of the dead (Satan) wholly irresistible, the Lord 'quickens' ('makes alive') all whom He chose in Christ Jesus before the foundation of the world. It is the gift of the New Nature which makes us find Jesus Christ absolutely 'irresistible'...The new nature which is a living human spirit, a new creation, in Christ, finds God irresistible as his formerly 'dead' human spirit once found the devil 'irresistible'" (Spencer 44, 45).

Let's Look At The Scriptures

1. How does Jesus say we will be drawn (John 6:44-45)? _____
_____

Calvin said in his commentary on John 6:44, "The statement amounts to this, that we ought not to wonder if many refuse to embrace the Gospel; because no man will ever of himself be able to come to Christ, but God must first approach him by his Spirit; and hence it follows that all are not drawn, but that God bestows this grace on those whom he has elected. True, indeed, as to the kind of drawing, it is not violent, so as to compel men by external force; but still it is a powerful impulse of the Holy Spirit, which makes men willing who formerly were unwilling and reluctant. It is a false and profane assertion, therefore, that none are drawn but those who are willing to be drawn, as if man made himself obedient to God by his own efforts; for the willingness with which men follow God is what they already have from himself, who has formed their hearts to obey him."

2. Who is the "natural man" and who is the "spiritual" man in 1 Cor. 2:14-15; 1:18-24?
_____
_____

    A. What has the Spirit revealed (1 Cor. 2:9-13)? _____
_____

    B. Where do we find this revelation? _____
_____

Calvin said in his commentary of 1 Cor. 2:14, "he draws a comparison between the animal man and the spiritual. As the latter denotes the man whose understanding is regulated by the illumination of the Spirit of God, there can be no doubt that the former denotes the man that is left in a purely natural condition, as they speak."

3. How did God open the heart of Lydia (Acts 16:14)? _____
_____

Calvin said in his commentary on Acts 16:14, "He had of late commended her godliness; and yet he showeth that she could not comprehend the doctrine of the gospel, save only through the illumination of the Spirit. Wherefore, we see that not faith alone, but all understanding and knowledge of spiritual things, is the peculiar gift of God, and that the ministers do no good by teaching and speaking unless the inward calling of God be thereunto added."

4. Is it possible to resist the Holy Spirit (Acts 7:51)? _____ How (Acts 7:52-53)?
_____

5. Paul said that God commands all men to repent (Acts 17:30-31). Is it possible to disobey a direct command of God? _____ How? _____
_____

6. In Acts 2, on the day of Pentecost, 3,000 people were saved. Answer the following questions to note what part the Holy Spirit had in their conversion.

   a. From where did the miracle of tongue speaking come and what was the reaction of the people (Acts 2:4-16)? _____
   _____

   b. Peter said, "Hear these words" (Acts 2:22). Where did these words come from and what reaction did the people have? _____
   _____

   c. When did they receive the Holy Spirit; before or after their conversion (Acts 2:38)?
   _____

   d. Who was saved: those who made a choice to receive the word spoken or those who had the Holy Spirit drive them to it (Acts 2:41)? _____
   _____

7. How are we "called" (2 Thess. 2:13-14)? _____
_____

8. How do we come to have faith (Rom. 10:17)? _____

9. Where did Paul say God's power to save man is found (Rom. 1:16)? _____
_____

PERSEVERANCE OF THE SAINTS (1)

As Defined By Calvinists

Perseverance of the Saints/Once Saved, Always Saved

Regarding perseverance of the saints, consider the following statements from the Westminster Confession of Faith.

I. They, whom God has accepted in His Beloved, effectually called, and sanctified by His Spirit, can neither totally nor finally fall away from the state of grace, but shall certainly persevere therein to the end, and be eternally saved (The Westminster Confession of Faith 74-75).

II. This perseverance of the saints depends not upon their own free will, but upon the immutability of the decree of election, flowing from the free and unchangeable love of God the Father; upon the efficacy of the merit and intercession of Jesus Christ, the abiding of the Spirit, and of the seed of God within them, and the nature of the covenant of grace: from all which arises also the certainty and infallibility thereof (The Westminster Confession of Faith 75-77).

III. Nevertheless, they may, through the temptations of Satan and of the world, the prevalence of corruption remaining in them, and the neglect of the means of their preservation, fall into grievous sins; and, for a time, continue therein: whereby they incur God's displeasure, and grieve His Holy Spirit, come to be deprived of some measure of their graces and comforts, have their hearts hardened, and their consciences wounded; hurt and scandalize others, and bring temporal judgments upon themselves. (The Westminster Confession of Faith 77-78)

I. Although hypocrites and other unregenerate men may vainly deceive themselves with false hopes and carnal presumptions of being in the favor of God, and estate of salvation (which hope of theirs shall perish): yet such as truly believe in the Lord Jesus, and love Him in sincerity, endeavouring to walk in all good conscience before Him, may, in this life, be certainly assured that they are in the state of grace, and may rejoice in the hope of the glory of God, which hope shall never make them ashamed (The Confession of Faith 79).

IV. True believers may have the assurance of their salvation divers ways shaken, diminished, and intermitted; as, by negligence in preserving of it, by falling into some special sin which wounds the conscience and grieves the Spirit; by some sudden or vehement temptation, by God's withdrawing the light of His countenance, and suffering even such as fear Him to walk in darkness and to have no light: yet are they never so utterly destitute of that seed of God, and life of faith, that love of Christ and the brethren, that sincerity of heart, and conscience of duty, out of which, by the operation of the Spirit, this assurance may, in due time, be revived; and by the which, in the mean time, they are supported from utter despair (The Westminster Confession of Faith 82).

"Not only does God choose certain ones to be delivered from their total depravity, provide for their salvation and purity, and effectually call them, but He also ordains the means for their preservation in their new life of holiness, righteousness and true knowledge. The indwelling Holy Spirit so preserves and enables that each of the elect most certainly endures to the end" (Green 4).

Let's Look At The Scriptures

1. What does the one who "hears" and "believes" have (John 5:24)? _____
_____

    a. Is it possible to stop hearing and believing and therefore stop having everlasting life? _____
_____

    b. Is it the life that is everlasting or our possession of that life? _____
_____

Calvin said in his commentary on John 5:24, "The meaning therefore is, that we are beyond the danger of death, because we are acquitted through the grace of Christ; and, therefore, though Christ sanctifies and regenerates us, by his Spirit, to newness of life, yet here he specially mentions the unconditional forgiveness of sins, in which alone the happiness of men consists."

2. What is the promise of Jesus in John 10:28? _____

    a. Who are the sheep of Jesus (John 10:26-27)? _____

    b. Is it possible to stop hearing and following Jesus? _____
_____

Calvin said in his commentary on John 10:28, "This is a remarkable passage, by which we are taught that the salvation of all the elect is not less certain than the power of God is invincible...Hence, too, we infer how mad is the confidence of the Papists, which relies on free-will, on their own virtue, and on the merits of their works. Widely different is the manner in which Christ instructs his followers, to remember that, in this world, they may be said to be in the midst of a forest, surrounded by innumerable robbers, and are not only unarmed and exposed as a prey, but are aware that the cause of death is contained in themselves, so that, relying on the guardianship of God alone, they may walk without alarm. In short, our salvation is certain, because it is in the hand of God; for our faith is weak, and we are too prone to waver."

3. What is God doing in us (Phil. 1:6)? _____

_____

    a. What does man have to do in order for God to continue to work in him (Phil. 2:12; 3:12)? _____

_____

Calvin said in his commentary on Phil. 1:6, "God is not like men, so as to be wearied out or exhausted by conferring kindness. Let, therefore, believers exercise themselves in constant meditation upon the favors which God confers, that they may encourage and confirm hope as to the time to come, and always ponder in their mind this syllogism: God does not forsake the work which his own hands have begun, as the Prophet bears witness, (Psalms 138:8; Isaiah 64:8) we are the work of his hands; therefore he will complete what he has begun in us."

4. Is it possible for some to be within the membership of a local church and not be truly converted (1 John 2:19)? _____

_____

    a. Is this true of everyone who falls away? _____

_____

Calvin said in his commentary on 1 John 2:19, "He does not speak here of the constancy of men, but of God, whose election must be ratified. He does not then, without reason declare, that where the calling of God is effectual, perseverance would be certain. He, in short, means that they who fall away had never been thoroughly imbued with the knowledge of Christ, but had only a light and a transient taste of it."

5. Is it possible to fall from grace (Gal. 5:4)? _____

    a. What does falling from grace mean? _____

_____

PERSEVERANCE OF THE SAINTS (2)

Let's Look at the Scriptures

1. Is it possible to be reconciled to God but lose one's salvation by not continuing to live by faith (Col. 1:21-23)? _____
_____

Calvin said in his commentary on Col. 1:23, "Here we have an exhortation to perseverance, by which he admonishes them that all the grace that had been conferred upon them hitherto would be vain, unless they persevered in the purity of the gospel. And thus he intimates, that they are still only making progress, and have not yet reached the goal. For the stability of their faith was at that time exposed to danger through the stratagems of the false apostles. Now he paints in lively colors assurance of faith when he bids the Colossians be grounded and settled in it. For faith is not like mere opinion, which is shaken by various movements, but has a firm steadfastness, which can withstand all the machinations of hell. Hence the whole system of Popish theology will never afford even the slightest taste of true faith, which holds it as a settled point, that we must always be in doubt respecting the present state of grace, as well as respecting final perseverance."

2. Is it possible for someone who partakes in the blessings in Christ to fall away (Heb. 6:4-6)? _____
_____

Calvin said in his commentary on Heb. 6:4, 6, "To all this I answer, that God indeed favors none but the elect alone with the Spirit of regeneration, and that by this they are distinguished from the reprobate; for they are renewed after his image and receive the earnest of the Spirit in hope of the future inheritance, and by the same Spirit the Gospel is sealed in their hearts. But I cannot admit that all this is any reason why he should not grant the reprobate also some taste of his grace, why he should not irradiate their minds with some sparks of his light, why he should not give them some perception of his goodness, and in some sort engrave his word on their hearts...There is therefore some knowledge even in the reprobate, which afterwards vanishes away, either because it did not strike roots sufficiently deep, or because it withers, being choked up...In short, the Apostle warns us, that repentance is not at the will of man, but that it is given by God to those only who have not wholly fallen away from the faith...But when any one rises up again after falling, we may hence conclude that he had not been guilty of defection, however grievously he may have sinned."

3. Is it possible to say we have fellowship with God and walk in darkness (1 John 1:5-7)?
_____

   a. What does it mean to "walk in the light?" _____
_____

   b. What should we do if we sin (1 John 1:8-10)? _____
_____

Calvin said in his commentary on 1 John 1:6,7, "This doctrine, however, depends on a higher principle, that God sanctifies all who are his. For it is not a naked precept that he gives, which requires that our life should be holy; but he rather shews that the grace of Christ serves for this end to dissipate darkness, and to kindle in us the light of God; as though he had said, 'What God communicates to us is not a vain fiction; for it is necessary that the power and effect of this fellowship should shine forth in our life; otherwise the possession of the gospel is fallacious.'"

4. Is it possible for someone to receive the word but later fall away (Matt. 13:20-21; Luke 8:13)? _____

Calvin said in his commentary on Matt. 13:21, "Such persons, according to Matthew and Mark, are temporary, (204) not only because, having professed, for a time, that they are the disciples of Christ, they afterwards fall away through temptation, but because they imagine that they have true faith...In a word, let us learn that none are partakers of true faith, except those who are sealed with the Spirit of adoption, and who sincerely call on God as their Father; and as that Spirit is never extinguished, so it is impossible that the faith, which he has once engraven on the hearts of the godly, shall pass away or be destroyed."

5. How did Peter describe the man who had "escaped the pollutions of the world through the knowledge of the Lord and Savior Jesus Christ" but became "entangled" again (2 Pet. 2:20-22)? _____
_____
_____

Calvin said in his commentary on 2 Pet. 2:20, "But he declares that they who make themselves slaves again to the pollutions of the world fall away from the gospel. The faithful also do indeed sin; but as they allow not dominion to sin, they do not fall away from the grace of God, nor do they renounce the profession of sound doctrine which they have once embraced. For they are not to be deemed conquered, while they strenuously resist the flesh and its lusts."

6. What is the consequence for the righteous man who turns to sin (Ezek. 18:24-26)?
_____

   a. Why does this sinner die? Is it God's fault? _____
_____

7. Discussion question: Does Calvinism bring assurance to the believer? Listen to Calvin's assurance, "Perseverance is the gift of God, which he dos not lavish promiscuously on all, but imparts to whom he pleases. If it is asked how the difference arises—why some steadily persevere, and others prove deficient in steadfastness - we can give no other reason than that the Lord, by his mighty power, strengthens and sustains the former, so that they perish not, while he does not furnish the same assistance to the latter, but leaves them to be monuments of instability" (Calvin "Institutes of the Christian Religions". Book 2, Chapter 5, No. 3, p 198). _____

_____

_____

_____

_____

IMPUTED RIGHTEOUSNESS

As Defined By Calvinists

"I reply that 'accepting grace,' as they call it, is nothing else than his free goodness, with which the Father embraces us in Christ when he clothes us with the innocence of Christ and accepts it as ours that by the benefit of it he may hold us as holy, pure, and innocent. For Christ's righteousness, which as it alone is perfect alone can bear the sight of God, must appear in court on our behalf, and stand surely in judgment. Furnished with this righteousness, we obtain continual forgiveness of sins in faith. Covered with this purity, the sordidness and uncleanness of our imperfection are not ascribed to us but are hidden as if buried that they may not come into God's judgment, until the hour arrives when, the old man slain and clearly destroyed in us, the divine goodness will receive us into blessed peace with the new Adam" (Calvin Institutes. Book 3, Chapter 14, No. 12, p 486).

"Thus we simply interpret justification, as the acceptance with which God receives us into his favor as if we were righteous; and we say that this justification consists in the forgiveness of sins and the imputation of the righteousness of Christ" (Calvin Institutes. Book 3, Chapter 11, No. 2, p 445).

> I. Those whom God effectually calls, He also freely justifies; not by infusing righteousness into them, [Catholicism JRA] but by pardoning their sins, and by accounting and accepting their persons as righteous; not for any thing wrought in them, or done by them, but for Christ's sake alone; nor by imputing faith itself, the act of believing, or any other evangelical obedience to them, as their righteousness; but by imputing the obedience and satisfaction of Christ unto them, they receiving and resting on Him and His righteousness by faith; which faith they have not of themselves, it is the gift of God (The Westminster Confession of Faith 50-51).

> III. Christ, by His obedience and death, did fully discharge the debt of all those that are thus justified, and did make a proper, real and full satisfaction to His Father's justice in their behalf. Yet, in as much as He was given by the Father for them; and His obedience and satisfaction accepted in their stead; and both, freely, not for any thing in them; their justification is only of free grace; that both the exact justice, and rich grace of God might be glorified in the justification of sinners (The Westminster Confession of Faith 52-53).

"Christ, acting on behalf of His people, perfectly kept God's law and thereby worked out a perfect righteousness which is imputed or credited to them the moment they are brought to faith in Him. Through what He did, they are constituted righteous before God. They are also freed from all guilt and condemnation as the result of what Christ suffered for them...They are saved, not because of what they themselves have done or will do, but solely on the ground of Christ's redeeming work" (Steele 39).

Let's Look At The Scriptures

1. In what sense did Jesus become our "wisdom from God—and righteousness and sanctification and redemption" (NKJV - 1 Cor. 1:30; 2 Cor. 5:21)? _____
_____

Calvin said in his commentary on 1 Cor. 1:30, "he says that he is made unto us righteousness, by which he means that we are on his account acceptable to God, inasmuch as he expiated our sins by his death, and his obedience is imputed (Calvin meant "transferred" when he used the word "imputed", JRA) to us for righteousness."

2. In what sense are we "saved by His life?" Is it His life before or after His resurrection (Rom. 5:10)? _____
_____

3. What was the "one act of righteousness" Jesus did and how does that make us righteous (Rom. 5:19)? _____
_____

Calvin said in his commentary on Rom. 5:19, "And then, as he declares that we are made righteous through the obedience of Christ, we hence conclude that Christ, in satisfying the Father, has provided a righteousness for us. It then follows, that righteousness is in Christ, and that it is to be received by us as what peculiarly belongs to him. He at the same time shows what sort of righteousness it is, by calling it obedience."

4. What contrast did Paul make between "not having my own righteousness" and "righteousness which is from God" (Phil. 3:9)? _____
_____

Calvin said in his commentary on Phil. 3:9, "He thus, in a general way, places man's merit in opposition to Christ's grace; for while the law brings works, faith presents man before God as naked, that he may be clothed with the righteousness of Christ. When, therefore, he declares that the righteousness of faith is from God, it is not simply because faith is the gift of God, but because God justifies us by his goodness, or because we receive by faith the righteousness which he has conferred upon us."

5. What does "impute" or "reckon" mean (Rom. 4:3, 22)? _____
_____

   a. Does Paul say that Christ's righteousness is imputed to us or that our faith is imputed as righteousness? _____

   b. What does that mean? _____
_____

Calvin said in his commentary on Rom. 4:6, "We hence conclude that the question is not, what men are in themselves, but how God regards them; not that purity of conscience and integrity of life are to be separated from the gratuitous favor of God; but that when the reason is asked, why God loves us and owns us as just, it is necessary that Christ should come forth as one who clothes us with his own righteousness."

6. As we have previously noted, the Calvinist believes that we inherit the original sin and a depraved/sinful nature. He believes forgiveness of original sin is not enough for our salvation. We must also have the sinless law-keeping and righteousness of Jesus to cover up our sinful nature. The truth is we need forgiveness for our sins and once these sins are forgiven, we are righteous.

   a. How does Paul describe the process of our salvation (Rom. 4:5-8)? _____
   _____
   _____

7. Is it possible for the righteousness of one person to be transferred to another (Ezek. 18:20)? _____

8. Did Jesus receive the punishment for our sins on the cross? When God looks at the forgiven Christian, does He see the punishment for his sins paid by Jesus (Heb. 2:9)? _____
   _____

9. Is there a passage that says that Jesus kept the law as our substitute? Is there any passage that says Jesus' sinless law-keeping is transferred to us? _____
   _____
   _____

FAITH ONLY (1)

As Defined By Calvinists

Faith Only

"But here also Scripture [Rom. 3:23-24] reclaims, simply affirming that Christ is both righteousness and life, and that the blessing of justification is possessed by faith alone" (Calvin Institutes. Book 3, Chapter 14, No. 17, p 481).

"In vain do they lay hold of the frivolous subtilty, that the faith alone, by which we are justified, "worketh by love," and that love, therefore, is the foundation of justification. We, indeed, acknowledge with Paul, that the only faith which justifies is that which works by love (Gal. 3:6); but love does not give it its justifying power. Nay, its only means of justifying consists in its bringing us into communication with the righteousness of Christ. Otherwise the whole argument, on which the Apostle insists with so much earnestness, would fall. 'To him that worketh is the reward not reckoned of grace, but of debt. But to him that worketh not, but believeth on him that justifieth the ungodly, his faith is counted for righteousness.' Could he express more clearly than in this word, that there is justification in faith only where there are no works to which reward is due, and that faith is imputed for righteousness only when righteousness is conferred freely without merit?" (Calvin Institutes. Book 3, Chapter 11, No. 20, p 460).

> I. The grace of faith, whereby the elect are enabled to believe to the saving of their souls, is the work of the Spirit of Christ in their hearts, and is ordinarily wrought by the ministry of the Word, by which also, and by the administration of the sacraments, and prayer, it is increased and strengthened (The Westminster Confession of Faith, Chapter XIV, Of Saving Faith).

Faith as Defined by Others

Lutheran

> 1. Faith without works is sufficient for salvation, and alone justifies.
> 2. Justifying faith is a sure trust, by which one believes that his sins are remitted for Christ's sake; and they that are justified are to believe certainly that their sins are remitted.

3. By faith only we are able to appear before God, who neither regards nor has need of our works; faith only purifying us.
4. No previous disposition is necessary to justification; neither does faith justify because it disposes us, but because it is a means or instrument by which the promise and grace of God are laid hold on and received.
5. All the works of men, even the most sanctified, are sin.

(Martin Luther as quoted from The Large Catechism)

"Faith is not what some people think it is. Their human dream is a delusion. Because they observe that faith is not followed by good works or a better life, they fall into error, even though they speak and hear much about faith. 'Faith is not enough,' they say, You must do good works, you must be pious to be saved'. They think that, when you hear the gospel, you start working, creating by your own strength a thankful heart which says, 'I believe.' That is what they think true faith is. But, because this is a human idea, a dream, the heart never learns anything from it, so it does nothing and reform doesn't come from this 'faith,' either. Instead, faith is God's work in us, that changes us and gives new birth from God (John 1:13). It kills the old Adam and makes us completely different people. It changes our hearts, our spirits, our thoughts and all our powers. It brings the Holy Spirit with it. Yes, it is a living, creative, active and powerful thing, this faith. Faith cannot help doing good works constantly. It doesn't stop to ask if good works ought to be done, but before anyone asks, it already has done them and continues to do them without ceasing. Anyone who does not do good works in this manner is an unbeliever. He stumbles around and looks for faith and good works, even though he does not know what faith or good works are. Yet he gossips and chatters about faith and good works with many words" (Luther, Commentary on Romans 16-17).

Methodist

"We are accounted righteous before God only for the merit of our Lord and Saviour Jesus Christ, by faith, and not for our own works or deservings. Wherefore, that we are justified by faith, only, is a most wholesome doctrine, and very full of comfort" (The Book of Discipline of the United Methodist Church, Article IX, Of the Justification of Man, p. 55).

Baptist

"We believe the Scriptures teach that the great gospel blessing which Christ secures to such as believe in him is justification; that justification includes the pardon of sin, and the gift of eternal life on principles of righteousness; that it is bestowed, not in consideration of any works of righteousness which we have done, but solely through faith in Christ; by means of which faith his perfect righteousness is freely imputed to us by God; that it brings us into a state of most blessed peace and favor with God, and secures every other blessing needed for times and eternity" (Hiscox 62).

Let's Look At The Scriptures

1. In John 3:16, Romans 5:1 and John 5:24, Jesus says that faith is necessary for salvation. Is Jesus saying that faith is the only condition of salvation? _____
   _____
   _____

2. "Believe" and "faith" come from the same Greek word. "Believe" is the translation of
   the verb and "faith" is the translation of the noun. What does this word mean? ____
   _____

3. In Romans 4, Paul used the faith of Abraham as an example of the type of faith that
   saves. Look through the following verses and discover the type of faith Abraham had.

   a. In Genesis 12:1, God told Abraham to leave Haran.
      How old was Abraham (Gen. 12:4)? _____
      What comment is made about Abraham in this time frame (Heb. 11:8)? _____
      _____

   b. In Genesis 15:6, God promised a son to Abraham and Abraham's faith was imputed
      as righteousness. Paul quoted this verse in Romans 4:3.
      How old was Abraham (Gen. 16:3)? _____
      What comment was made about Abraham in this time frame (Rom. 4:1-5)? ____
      _____

   c. In Romans 4:22, Paul quoted Genesis 15:6 again but this time applied it to another
      time in Abraham's life.
      How old was Abraham (Rom. 4:19)? _____
      What were the circumstances (Rom. 4:16-22, Gen. 17:16-19; 21:1-5)? _____
      _____
      What connection is made between Abraham's faith and ours (Rom. 4:23-25)? __
      _____

   d. In James 2:23, James quoted Genesis 15:6 again and applied it to another time in
      Abraham's life.
      What were the circumstances (James 2:21-23, Gen. 22:1-14)? _____
      _____
      About how old was Abraham? _____

   e. What can we learn about faith from the example of Abraham given to us by
      God? _____
      _____

FAITH ONLY (2)

Let's Look At The Scriptures

1. What is the answer to the question in James 2:14? _____

_____

Martin Luther, in his Preface to the Epistles of St. James and St. Jude, said, "I think highly of the epistle of James,...Yet to give my own opinion, without prejudice to that of anyone else, I do not hold it to be of apostolic authorship. First, in direct opposition to Paul and the rest of the Bible, it ascribes justification to works, quoting Abraham wrongly as one who was justified by his works...He does violence to Scripture, and so contradicts Paul and all Scripture. He tries to accomplish by emphasizing law what the apostles bring about by attracting man to love. I therefore refuse him a place among the writers of the true canon of my Bible" (Barclay 7).

Calvin said in his commentary on James 2:20, "We must understand the state of the question, for the dispute here is not respecting the cause of justification, but only what avails a profession of faith without works, and what opinion we are to form of it. Absurdly then do they act who strive to prove by this passage that man is justified by works, because James meant no such thing, for the proofs which he subjoins refer to this declaration, that no faith, or only a dead faith, is without works...The Sophists lay hold on the word justified, and then they cry out as being victorious, that justification is partly by works. But we ought to seek out a right interpretation according to the general drift of the whole passage. We have already said that James does not speak here of the cause of justification, or of the manner how men obtain righteousness, and this is plain to every one; but that his object was only to shew that good works are always connected with faith; and, therefore, since he declares that Abraham was justified by works, he is speaking of the proof he gave of his justification.

"When, therefore, the Sophists set up James against Paul, they go astray through the ambiguous meaning of a term. When Paul says that we are justified by faith, he means no other thing than that by faith we are counted righteous before God. But James has quite another thing in view, even to shew that he who professes that he has faith, must prove the reality of his faith by his works. Doubtless James did not mean to teach us here the ground on which our hope of salvation ought to rest; and it is this alone that Paul dwells upon."

2. What is faith without works (James 2:17,20)? _____

3. James said that demons believe (James 2:19). Are they saved? If not, why not? ___
_____

4. Define "worketh" as used in James 2:24. _____
_____

Calvin said in his commentary on James 2:23, "Why then does James say that it was fulfilled? Even because he intended to shew what sort of faith that was which justified Abraham; that is, that it was not idle or evanescent, but rendered him obedient to God, as also we find in Hebrews 11:8. The conclusion, which is immediately added, as it depends on this, has no other meaning. Man is not justified by faith alone, that is, by a bare and empty knowledge of God; he is justified by works, that is, his righteousness is known and proved by its fruits."

5. Define "works" as used in Rom. 4:5. _____
_____

6. What was necessary for the Philippian jailor to do to be saved (Acts 16:31-33)? ___
_____

7. What is necessary for someone to become a Christian (Mark 16:15-16; Acts 2:36-41; Eph. 2:8-10)? (Please use any other verses you wish.) _____
_____
_____

   a. Is this something in opposition to or in harmony with faith? _____
_____

8. What is necessary for us to be forgiven of sin after we become a Christian (Acts 8:21-22; 1 John 1:8-10)? _____
_____

   a. Is this something in opposition to or in harmony with faith? _____
_____

Works Cited

Bainton, Roland. *HERE I STAND: A Life of Martin Luther.* New York: Penguin Group, 1997. Print.

Barclay, William. *The Letter of James.* Philadelphia: Westminster, 1976. Print.

Boettner, Lorraine. "The Sovereignty of God" *The Sword and Trowel.* May/June, Plano Texas: Multi-Communication Ministries, Inc. 1982.

Boettner, Lorraine. *The Reformed Faith.* Theologue.wordpress.com. 2012.

Boettner, Lorraine. *The Reformed Doctrine of Predestination.* 1939.

Calvin, John. "Institutes of the Christian Religion." *Christian Classics Ethereal Library.* (http://www.ccel.org/ccel/calvin/institutes.html).

Catechism of the Catholic Church, 2nd ed. Washington D.C., 1994.

Center for Reformed Theology and Apologetics. www.reformed.org.

Church of the Nazarene Manual. Kansas City: Nazarene Publishing House. 1976.

Farrar, Dean Frederic. *History of Interpretation,* London: Macmillan and Co., 1886 (http://www.preteristarchive.com/Books/pdf/1886_farrar_history-of-interpretation.pdf).

Green, Jay. *Calvinism: Yesterday, Today and Tomorrow!.* 1968. (original contents found in The Encyclopedia of Christianity, II in article entitled, Calvinism).

Hiscox, Edward. *The Standard Manual for Baptist Churches.* Philadelphia: American Baptist, 1890.

Jacobs, Alan. *Original Sin.* New York NY: HarperCollins, 2001.

Luther, Martin. *Commentary on Romans.* Grand Rapids: Kregel, 1954.

Manual of the Christian and Missionary Alliance. 2017.

Pink, Arthur. *The Sovereignty of God.* (http://www.pbministries.org/books/pink/Sovereignty/index.htm).

Revell, John. "Calvinism - Southern Baptist Perspectives" *SBCLII Journal of the Southern Baptist.* October 2010

Singer, C. Gregg. *John Calvin, His Roots and Fruits,* N. J., 1967.

Spencer, Duane. Tulip: The Five Points of Calvinism in the Light of Scripture. Grand Rapids: Baker. 1979

Statement of Fundamental and Essential Truths Pentecostal Assemblies of Canada. 2014.

Steele, David N. and Thomas, Curtis C. *The Five Points of Calvinism, Defined, Defended, Documented.* Presbyterian and Reformed Publishing Co., 1975.

The Book of Discipline of the United Methodist Church. Nashville: United Methodist Publishing.

Wesley, Alice Blair. *Our Unitarian Universalist Faith: Frequently Asked Questions.* (http://www.uuabookstore.org/Assets/PDFs/3017.pdf).

www.ingramcontent.com/pod-product-compliance
Lightning Source LLC
Chambersburg PA
CBHW081251040426
42452CB00015B/2787